CHARISMA

34 Tricks to Unlock Your Charisma,
Master the Art of Small Talk and
Develop Personal Magnetism

Akash P. Karia

#1 Internationally Bestselling Author of
"Small Talk Hacks" and
"How Successful People Think Differently"
www.AkashKaria.com

BESTSELLING BOOKS BY AKASH KARIA

Available on Amazon (www.bit.ly/AkashKaria):

Small Talk Hacks

How to Deliver a Great TED Talk

How to Design TED-Worthy Presentation Slides

Own the Room: Presentation Techniques to Keep Your Audience on the Edge of Their Seats

ANTI Negativity: How to Stop Negative Thinking and Lead a Positive Life

Persuasion Psychology: 26 Powerful Techniques to Persuade Anyone!

How Successful People Think Differently

Free Resources

There are hundreds of free articles as well as several eBooks, MP3s and videos on Akash's blog. To get instant access to those, head over to www.AkashKaria.com.

RAVE REVIEWS FOR "CHARISMA"

"**2X your networking results by reading this book!** I very much enjoyed reading this book. Quick read with a lot of practical [tools]. If you want learn how to develop instant rapport, you need to read this book."
~ Leo Landaverde

"*CHARISMA: 34 Little Tricks to Unlock Your Inner Charisma* is an excellent read! Clear, concise information in a bite-sized guide. Well written in a manner that keeps the reader's attention. The takeaways are highly relevant and usable in every day life. I will definitely re-read and keep this **valuable resource as my "go to" guide!**"
~ Ellen W

"If everyone read this book and followed the exercises the world would be a better place. I particularly like the areas around likeability and authenticity. **Highly recommended!**"
~ Diane Hope

"Akash Karia has written **a 5 star book on how to be charismatic.** In this book, Akash [shares] traits you need to develop in your everyday interactions with others to get them to like you, to want to know you better, to want to be with you. The tools he shares are invaluable if you want to get ahead in business and social settings.

Akash talks about your body language, how to ask the right kind of questions, how to be an active listener, how to be interesting [and] plus a lot more. I highly recommend this book!"
~ Allan Kaufman, DTM, Bestselling Author of *NLP: A Self-Help Guide to Personal Achievement & Influence*

"**Yet another homerun!** This is the 6th book I have read from this author. He has an excellent way of taking complicated concepts and reducing them to succinct and understandable chunks of USABLE information. This book, like his others, is no different. He takes something essential and fundamental to success and writes in a manner anyone can understand.... and implement. Get this book...and check out all his others, you won't be disappointed."
~ Eric Laughton, Certified John Maxwell Coach, Bestselling Author of *From Coma to Competition*

CONTENTS

YOUR FREE GIFT

As a way of saying thank you for your purchase, I'd like to offer you a free bonus package worth $297. This bonus package contains eBooks, videos and audiotapes on how master the art of persuasion, become a great public speaker and develop your charisma. You can download the free bonus here:
www.AkashKaria.com/FREE

WHAT PEOPLE SAY ABOUT AKASH KARIA

Akash Karia is a peak performance coach who has trained over 50,000 people worldwide, from bankers in Hong Kong to senior executives in Thailand to government members in Dubai.

"Akash is a wonderful professional speaker who has a great message, is motivating, inspiring and interactive at the same time, so if you're thinking of hiring a speaker for any reason at any time, please be sure to hire Akash because he'll do a wonderful job for you!"
~ **Brian Tracy, CPAE Speaker Hall of Fame, #1 Bestselling Author of *Maximum Achievement***

"Akash is a very effective, inspiring and energetic speaker!"
~ **Azim Jamal, Nautilus Gold Award Winner,**

"Akash is a phenomenal coach! The information I gained in just a few short hours is priceless."
Fatema Dewji, Director of Marketing for billion-dollar conglomerate, MeTL Tanzania

Subject to availability, Akash conducts keynotes, workshops and seminars internationally. Get in touch with him on www.AkashKaria.com/Speaking (or via Akash@AkashKaria.com).

Chapter One

THE ONE QUALITY THE MOST SUCCESSFUL PEOPLE HAVE IN COMMON – AND HOW YOU CAN GET IT TOO

"Charisma is a sparkle in people that money can't buy. It's an invisible energy with visible effects."

Marianne Williamson

If there is one secret ingredient to success, it has to be charisma. If you think of the most successful people on the planet, you would be hard-pressed to find many who have not mastered the art of charisma.

But what is this magical ingredient called charisma?

If you asked 100 people, the most likely answer you would get is that charisma is that special something – the magnetism or charm that draws others in. However, almost all of those 100 people would struggle to define charisma or to explain what makes one person charismatic and another one not. But odds are every one of those 100 people would agree that when it comes to charisma, you know it when you see it.

A SPECIAL, MAGICAL QUALITY

Looking at the official dictionary definition of charisma, it is easy to see why we struggle so hard to define this personal quality even though we can always point it out when it is present.

In many definitions, charisma is considered to be a quality handed down from the heavens. The word "charisma" comes from the Greek words for "favor" and "grace." It is defined as a "special" quality, a "magical" quality, something magnetic that inspires loyalty, creates enthusiasm, and simply makes someone more appealing. It's no wonder people struggle to put the essence of charisma into words when it is so ethereal and magical that it seems to be a gift from the gods.

CAN THIS MAGICAL QUALITY BE TRAINED?

But, what if you aren't one of those people who are naturally charismatic? Does this mean you are doomed to lurk in the shadows of someone else's spotlight forever? Thankfully, no!

In fact, research indicates that while charisma does come naturally to some people, even those who aren't born with the ability to inspire an entire country to put a man on the moon with a single speech like John F. Kennedy can learn to be charismatic.

Experts estimate that only about half of the charisma of even the most charismatically gifted among us is innate. This is good news for the rest of us because it means charisma, like any other skill, is something we can be trained in, something time and effort can improve.

MY STORY

I have experienced great benefits in both my personal and professional life as a result of mastering the art of charisma.

When I was in high school, I was painfully shy. I was the boy who sat at the back of the class and rarely spoke to anyone. At lunch times, I would normally eat alone. I remember one particularly painful event when some of the kids in class decided to hold an after-school end-of-year party – and I was the only kid in class who didn't receive an invitation. I wish I could say I was exaggerating, but I'm not.

Fast-forward to today and I now lead an active social life. I have a group of close friends, I get along very well with my colleagues – and yes, I get invited to parties. I even landed the job as Chief Commercial Officer of a multimillion-dollar company based on the fact that I'm able to build strong relationships and networks with clients.

So, how was I able to make this transformation?

By learning as much as I could about the art of charisma – by learning how to master small talk, my mindset, and my body language. I read a great number of books on persuasion and influence and studied hundreds of DVDs and audio programs on how to develop a more magnetic personality.

I gradually implemented the techniques I learned into my life. I would take a particular technique and set myself a challenge to apply it to my life each week. Over a year, I became a more confident, approachable, and yes, even slightly charismatic individual.

The point is, it doesn't matter who you are or where you want to go in life, building t "muscles" can benefit anyone because it want to know us and to be around us. T that charismatic people make the space they inhab better place to be simply by being there. They are positive and uplifting and empowering, and they inspire us. They make us feel good simply by sharing their space. Even if you do not aspire to fame or celebrity, becoming more charismatic can reap real benefits in every area of your life.

HOW TO MAKE THE LEAP FROM FORGETTABLE TO FASCINATING

You may be wondering how you can make that leap and go from shadow-lurker to spotlight-grabber, from boring to bewitching, forgettable to fascinating. The answer is easy. You simply need to understand the characteristics highly charismatic people share, learn how to use the building blocks of charisma to incorporate those characteristics into your life, and then practice them until they become part of your personality.

In this book, you are going to learn how to become a more charismatic individual by adopting the traits of charismatic people. You will learn how to:

Portray confidence and charisma by mastering your body language.

- Establish rapport with almost anyone by using five simple techniques.

- Become a more likable person.

- Create an instant bond with anyone by becoming an active listener.

- Allow your authentic self to shine through.

I believe that if you master these five qualities – confidence, rapport building, likability, active listening, and authenticity – then you will become a more charismatic individual that people naturally want to be around.

Ready to unleash you inner charisma?

Then let's get started...

Chapter Two

HOW TO MASTER YOUR BODY LANGUAGE

"Charm is the quality in others that makes us
more satisfied with ourselves."
Henri Frederic Amiel

Think about the last time you met someone new.

Were you drawn to them?

Did they pique your interest?

Did you like them immediately?

Now think about how long it took you to form your initial impression of them. Research says it's likely your first impression was set in less than a second.

Take a minute to let that sink in…that means that most of the people you interact with are forming their impression of you before you speak a single word and, possibly, before you even realize they are sizing you up. This underlines the importance of sending the right nonverbal signals if you want to make a stellar first impression.

Your body language can make or break you when it comes to charisma, and gaining mastery over it is one of the most important skills you will need to develop as you work to become more charismatic.

JIM CARREY: A CASE STUDY IN BODY LANGUAGE

If you want to understand the power of body language, there is no better role model than Jim Carrey, who is known for his comedic antics on screen. His elastic face and body can communicate volumes without him having to utter a single word, and that is the true force behind his fame. His expert abilities in physical comedy stem from a mastery of body language.

Although often exaggerated, his facial expressions and body movements make us laugh because they are authentic. We see enough of ourselves in the quirky characters he plays to feel connected to them. This is the essence of body language: the ability to convey emotion, information, and meaning simply by moving a hand or nodding a head.

Don't worry, we'll dive deeper into body language in the next few techniques...

MASTERING BODY LANGUAGE

When you walk into a room full of new people, how do you decide who to approach? Who to talk to? Who is worth engaging with?

Body language.

You choose who you will engage with based on the nonverbal cues each person is sending out.

If someone is standing across from you with their arms crossed, your internal radar is likely to steer clear of them because having their arms crossed says "I am not open to meeting someone new."

If someone watches you walk in and then turns away without acknowledging you, you aren't likely to approach them either because the message they just sent was "not worth my time."

So, who should you seek out?

The person who looks up, catches your eye, and gives you a genuine smile. That person, without saying a word, acknowledges your existence, establishes a connection, and then tries to make you feel welcome with a smile.

While Jim Carrey's body language is generally over the top, most of the body language we experience every day is much more subtle. Charismatic people understand these subtleties and know what to do to send the message they want to send. They are fluent in body language and know how to use everything from their facial expression to the position of their arms to communicate with those around them.

Let's say you walk into that room full of people you don't know.

Do you know what kinds of messages your body is sending?

Are you choosing the messages your body is sending based on your reason for entering that room?

If the answer to either question is no, here are some ways that you can begin mastering those messages:

Body Language Tip #1:
CHARM THEM WITH INVITING EYES

In most of your interactions with others, the first thing you do is establish eye contact. And the type of eye contact you offer sets the stage for their impression of you and for the rest of the interaction.

EYE CONTACT

- If your eye contact is inviting, others will feel welcomed and drawn in.

- If your eye contact is aggressive or insistent, others will feel wary and may become guarded.

- If your eye contact is weak or nonexistent, others will feel that you aren't interested in them or in what they are saying.

The importance of offering the right eye contact cannot be overstated. Eye contact is more than just a social convention. In fact, it is one of the most important ways humans connect with each other. Simply looking directly into another person's eyes produces a biological reaction that our brain interprets as affection.

So, if you want to make a stellar first impression, start by improving your eye contact skills. If you find that making eye contact is difficult for you, here are some things to try the next time you are at a networking event or other social gathering:

A – THE EYE COLOR TECHNIQUE

The next time you are networking with new people, focus on figuring out the color of the person's eyes. This is one of my favorite tricks for making eye contact – it forces me to pay closer attention and make deeper eye contact with the other person, which leads to us feeling more connected. Try it because this little trick will help you get in the habit of making great eye contact right off the bat and because it is mission oriented, it can help alleviate the awkwardness some people feel when making eye contact.

B – RIGHT BETWEEN THE EYES

If looking directly into someone's eyes makes you extremely uncomfortable, focus on a spot right between their eyes. This will alleviate some of your discomfort while still making the connection with the other person.

However, over time, focus on becoming more comfortable with making direct eye contact with the other person. When this happens, the brain registers the contact and produces chemicals that make both parties feel more connected to each other.

C – OUT OF FOCUS

Another way to make eye contact if it makes you feel uncomfortable is to let your gaze go slightly out of focus. This will also alleviate some of the discomfort you are feeling without impeding the actual eye contact the other person is experiencing.

D – START WITH A SECOND

When first attempting to capture someone's gaze across the room at a party, or even in line at the grocery store, limit the initial contact to one or two seconds and then reinitiate a few seconds later. This ensures you are making the impression you want without coming off like a stalker.

E – IF AT FIRST YOU DON'T SUCCEED…

Don't be afraid to attempt eye contact more than once when meeting someone new. We are all afraid of rejection, which makes us tentative when it comes to making the connection eye contact initiates. If you attempt to make eye contact and the other person looks away, try again.

F – BUT DON'T GO FOR THE THIRD STRIKE

After two tries, move on to someone else. Repeated attempts to initiate contact with someone who isn't receptive will seem aggressive and creepy, no matter what social setting you are in.

G – MIRROR THEM TO MAKE THEM COMFORTABLE…

Different people have different levels of comfort with eye contact, which means the "right" number of seconds to hold someone's gaze is going to vary from person to person.

The best way to ensure you are making the impression you want is to mirror the other person with a slight delay. This means that when they look at you, wait a slight moment, and then return their gaze. Then, when they look away, wait momentarily before doing the same.

H – EXCEPT WHEN EMOTIONS ARE INVOLVED

There is one circumstance where the mirroring tactic does not apply, and that is when you are having an emotional conversation. People struggle to talk about their emotions, and while this isn't something you are likely to have to deal with at a networking event or social outing, it is an important nuance you need to understand to master meaningful eye contact.

Because your goal is to build relationships, emotional conversations will be involved at some point. In these circumstances, do not mirror the other person when they look away. Odds are they are looking away because of the emotional context of the conversation, not because the eye contact feels weird. If you also look away, you will send a different message than you intend.

In fact, looking away when someone is sharing something emotional says "I don't care" and "I am not interested" or "This is making me uncomfortable." All of those messages will degrade and damage the relationship you are building. If your goal is to be supportive, keep your eyes on them, even if they look away. This lets them know that you care and in turn makes the other person like you more.

I – ONE THOUGHT, ONE PERSON TECHNIQUE

So far, these are all techniques to help you make eye contact when you are speaking one on one. But what if you are speaking to a group of people (as you often are in networking events or parties)?

One way to effectively manage eye contact when you are speaking to a group is to pick one person to make eye contact with at the start of each new thought. As you move from one thought or point to another, shift to a new person. This will make everyone feel included and will keep you from looking at one person for too long, from looking at the floor, or from letting your gaze wander aimlessly.

Remember, charismatic people make everyone in the group feel involved and engaged.

Body Language Tip #2:
PERFECTING YOUR POSTURE

Apart from eye contact, another way charismatic people exhibit their confidence, openness, and presence is through their posture.

Posture is the way you carry yourself, hold your body and move through space. Your posture is a critical part of your body language. It can convey everything from personality traits like confidence and strength to emotions like sadness or excitement.

In order to send the nonverbal messages you want to send when you walk into a room or take a seat at the table, you need to understand how your posture affects people's perception of you. Once you understand the posture-perception connection, you can use it to your advantage.

Here is how posture affects perception and what you can do to let everyone in the room know you are confident, capable, and charismatic.

A – STAND UP STRAIGHT

If you want people to believe you are confident and charismatic, check your posture. When people are self-confident it shows in the way they carry themselves. They stand up straight and tall and they hold their head high.

If you struggle with self-confidence issues, pay particular attention to your posture and how you stand. Any time you enter a room, focus on standing straight and tall with your shoulders back and your head high. Practice in the mirror so you get used to how it feels to stand and walk this way.

I personally realized I had a posture problem when I was at college. As part of my business communication course, our professor videotaped our presentations and made us watch the video. When I saw myself on video, I realized just how terrible my posture was! I was standing with my back rounded and my shoulders hunched forward which came across as a very unconfident and unattractive posture.

After realizing this, I made a conscious decision to stand straight. To this day, whenever I catch myself standing hunched over, I push my shoulders back, thrust my chest out ever so slightly and straighten up my back. Not only does this make me appear taller, it comes across as confident and self-assured, which are traits that all charismatic individuals embody.

B – SIT UP STRAIGHT TOO

Posture is also important when you are sitting down.

Imagine you are standing at the front of the room giving a presentation and you notice that one of the attendees is slouched over in their chair with their arms across their chest.

What message are they sending by sitting that way?

They are saying (through their body language), "I don't believe you, I don't care enough to pay attention, I am not open to what you have to say."

What about the message the woman on the other side of the table, who is hunched over the table, looking down and doodling on a piece of paper, is sending?

She's saying, "I am bored, I am not listening at all, I wish I wasn't here."

Now think about the messages you are getting from the person sitting closer to the front who is sitting up straight, making eye contact, taking notes, and nodding and smiling as they listen to you speak.

That person is saying, "I am interested, I am engaged, I care about what you are saying."

How you sit when interacting with others is an important part of how they will perceive you. Follow these rules whenever you are seated at a meeting, a dinner, on a date, or in any social environment where perception matters.

- Don't slouch.

- Don't lean away from the person. Instead, lean forward and towards them.

- If you need to take notes (such as in a business meeting), make sure you are looking up from those notes often enough to remain engaged in what others are saying.

- Maintain a connection with any others at the table or anyone speaking through focused attention, eye contact, and a smile.

Body Language Tip #3:
MASTER THE HANDSHAKE

It might seem a bit old-fashioned, but a solid handshake remains an important nonverbal communication tool that tells people a lot about you. Every time you shake hands, whether it is with a new business acquaintance at a networking event, a new love interest, or a potential employer, you need to know the message you want to send and then shake hands in a way that sends it.

Different handshakes send different messages.

- A weak handshake says, "I am weak, you won't be able to rely on me."

- A grip that is too tight, a handshake that is too forceful or that lasts too long all say, "I am overcompensating for something."

- A firm grip implies a strong character and self-confidence.

- A loose grip implies a lack of character.

Here are the four unwritten rules of giving a good handshake:

1 – When you find yourself in a social situation where you need to shake hands with someone new, always put your hand out first. This shows openness and confidence.

2 – Grip the other person's hand firmly, as you would grip something that is breakable but that you don't want to drop. Avoid bone-crushing grips, which don't make you seem strong or confident. Instead, they make you look like a bully with something to prove.

3 – A solid handshake lasts for only two or three pumps. Prolonging it makes you seem aggressive or creepy.

4 – Shake from the elbow, not the shoulder. You want your handshake to impart an aura of strength, competence, and confidence, not brute force.

It is as important to know when to shake hands, as it is to know how to shake hands, because defying this social convention can be as detrimental as doing it wrong. Always shake hands when you are introduced to someone new or when you introduce yourself to someone new. Shake hands when someone introduces themselves to you. During formal situations, shake hands at the end of the conversation.

If you aren't sure how to give a solid handshake, practice with a friend or family member. Then, practice whenever you can at every social event, networking get-together, business meeting, etc.

Body Language Tip #4:
ADOPT PROPER POSITIONING

Another aspect of body language is body and arm position.

If you are standing or sitting in a way that your body is exposed and open, the message you send is that you are open. Simply keeping the front of your body accessible says, "I am friendly. I am willing to meet new people. I am open to new things."

The opposite is true if you stand or sit in a way that blocks your body such as crossing your arms over your chest, crossing your legs, or slouching. All of these positions send negative messages like "I am anxious. I am not friendly. I have no interest in you or anything you have to say."

When you are interacting with others, keep your back straight, your arms uncrossed, and your torso exposed. Simply adopting this as your main body position in social situations will make you seem approachable, friendly, and willing to make new connections.

Body Language Tip #5:
RESPECT PERSONAL SPACE

If you have ever been standing at a bar or on a subway where there were a lot of people and a limited amount of space, you understand why personal space is an important aspect of body language.

Everyone needs a buffer zone around them in order to feel comfortable. When someone forces their way into that buffer zone, that person comes across as aggressive, untrustworthy, and even dangerous.

The bottom line is that the amount of physical distance you leave between you and a new acquaintance sends very powerful messages, and you need to understand those messages so that you don't send the wrong one.

Research indicates that there are four basic levels of personal space:

- Public

- Social

- Personal

- Intimate

At each of these levels, there is a specific amount of space required for that buffer zone. Basically, the closer your relationship, the more comfortable you will feel being physically closer to the other person.

Because the ramifications of violating personal space can be so damaging at the beginning of a relationship, you need to know how close is too close and when you can move closer.

Here is a breakdown of public and social personal space conventions:

PUBLIC

When interacting with the general public, most people prefer a buffer zone of 12 to 25 feet. This doesn't mean that you need 12 to 25 feet between you and some stranger on the street. It means when interacting with someone you don't know, this is a distance at which most people feel comfortable. It is most applicable to presentations and speaking engagements.

To understand this better, consider how you would feel if you were standing at the front of a room giving a speech to a bunch of people you don't know, and someone came and stood 5 or 6 feet away from you. For most people, this would feel strange and uncomfortable, and everyone would be wondering why someone had moved so close to you. You might even feel threatened, as if they had moved closer in order to argue with you or attack you.

The next time you are at an event with a public speaker, make note of the distance between where the speaker stands and the first row of seating. Odds are it will fall in the range of 12 to 25 feet.

SOCIAL

In situations where we are interacting with people we are acquainted with but that we don't know well, most of us prefer a distance of 4 to 6 feet. The length and type of our acquaintance will dictate where each person falls within that range.

Think about the way you interact with coworkers, friends of friends, people you met at a previous networking event, or service providers like the UPS guy. All of these kinds of relationships fall into this level.

From a charisma perspective, this is the most important level for you to understand because most of the people you interact with in social situations will fit here. When you first meet someone new, other than a potential romantic interest, follow these rules to ensure you don't violate their personal space unintentionally.

1 – Give them at least 4 feet of personal space after shaking their hand.

2 – Pay attention to their behavior. If they are leaning away from you, take a step back. Similarly, if they seemed to have positioned their body so that the front of their torso is turned away from you, then move back. These are all signs that they are uncomfortable with how close you are to them.

3 – Hold off on hugs, back slaps, or putting your arm around anyone you don't know very well until you are sure you have developed a good level of rapport with them.

Now, with that being said, the rules with potential romantic partners are not so cut-and-dry. When you first meet someone new, it is a good idea to follow the rules above. If, over the course of that initial meeting, you have a long conversation and begin developing a bond, it is normal to move closer together. Your job is to pay attention to their body language and to watch for the signs that you are getting too close outlined above.

Understanding personal space is critical to developing your charisma because charismatic people draw others in and make them feel comfortable and important. Violating personal space norms does the opposite of that and can undo all the other work you have done to improve your charisma.

Body Language Tip #6:
MASTER GESTURES AND HAND MOVEMENTS

Whether you are known to gesture wildly when you talk or reserve hand movements for important moments where emphasis is required, you are sending a message every time you move your hands.

Charismatic people understand the power of the gesture and consciously use it to the best effect. They are not the people who can't seem to talk without moving their hands, and their hand movements and gestures are never distracting. They understand that, just like the other kinds of body language, they way you move your hands and you head means something to other people and it isn't always the meaning you want to convey.

In order to master your own movements, you need to understand the messages sent by these universal gestures.

When you are talking, here's what various hand gestures and positions say:

- **Hands that are hidden** – Tells people they can't trust you. This is why I advise people to avoid keeping both hands in their pockets when they are talking to someone

- **Hands that never move while talking** – Tells people you aren't passionate, that you are indifferent or don't care about what you are talking about.

- **Hands open and gesturing naturally while you speak** – Tells people you are open, honest, and trustworthy.

- **Hands open and palms facing down** – Tells people you know what you are talking about, though it does portray authority and dominance.

- **Hands open and palms facing up** – Tells people that you are open and receptive to them.

- **Hands that are gesturing quickly** – Tells people you are excited, interested, and passionate about what you are saying.

- **Hands gesturing beyond the outline of the body** – Tells people you are expressing a big idea.

- **Hands gesturing wildly** – Tells people you are out of control.

- **Steepled hands, palms facing each other with fingertips touching** – Tells people you are an expert on the topic you are discussing.

- **Hands clasped in front of your body** – Tells people you are nervous, anxious, and insecure.

- **Touching your face, hair, or neck** – Tells people you are unsure of yourself and what you are saying.

Now that you understand the basics, take a few minutes to think about what kind of gestures and hand movements you use when interacting with someone new.

Are you a "hand talker"?

When you go to a networking event, where do you usually put your hands?

Pay attention to your hand movements and gestures for a whole day and see how often you are sending messages you don't mean to send. Then practice using more confident, self-assured movements in the mirror until they feel comfortable.

When you attend the next social gathering, focus on using your gestures and hand movements to reinforce the messages you are sending:

- If you want people to think you are open, honest, and approachable, use hand movements that leave your hand open and at an angle.

- If you want to convey that you are experienced or an expert on some topic, steeple your hands when you speak and watch how people react.

- Avoid clasping your hands behind your back or in front of you so you don't undermine the self-confidence you are trying to project.

- Try to avoid touching your hair or face while speaking to avoid coming across as insecure.

Using your hands and your head to make important points, to tell people you are listening, and to convey that you are open, honest, and experienced will automatically boost your charisma in almost any social situation.

The final aim of this exercise is not to get you to rehearse your hand gestures, but to get you into a position where you gesture naturally and confidently.

But, how do you know if your hand gestures are natural? Simple. If you have to think about what to do with your hands, then you are not using them naturally.

Instead of focusing too much on yourself (and your hands), focus on the other person. Forget about yourself and focus on the other person – and the hand gestures will come naturally to you. Every now and then, you can monitor your hand gestures and posture, but overall you want to forget about you and focus on the other person. When you do this, the other person will feel listened to and cared about, and thus begin to develop affectionate feelings towards you.

Body Language Tip #7:
SMILE… ALL THE WAY TO YOUR EYES

This is important enough to mention again. A sincere smile is one of your best nonverbal communication tools. It signifies openness and makes the person you are smiling at feel important. It is inviting and welcoming and can be an effective way to break the ice with someone new.

The sincere smile should look and feel different, even to you. Most people offer fake smiles where their lips move but their eyes don't portray the warmth and affection that a real smile carries.

So, how do you offer a *genuine* smile? The trick is to find something you like about the person. Be interested in the other person. Be excited about the magic that takes place when two individuals bond. Tap into the positive feelings of excitement, interest, and fun that are involved when meeting someone, and your smile will come naturally.

Once you know how to offer a genuine smile, get out there and see what it does for you in social interactions.

Make sure you smile that smile when you are shaking hands with someone, when initiating or sustaining eye contact with someone, and even simply when entering a room. You will be surprised at the way people react to you when you offer them a genuine and sincere smile.

IN A NUTSHELL

tice mastering your body language in social situations like networking events, bars, parties, etc., by doing the following:

- Making meaningful eye contact.

- Perfecting your posture.

- Choosing your gestures and hand movements carefully.

- Smiling.

Chapter Three

ESTABLISHING UNBREAKABLE RAPPORT WITH ALMOST ANYONE – ANY TIME

"The most effective way to achieve right relations with any living thing is to look for the best in it, and then help that best into the fullest expression."
Allen J. Boone

Rapport is the common ground we are all looking for and it is an essential building block of charisma. As previously mentioned, we are all seeking connections with other people with whom we share common ground. We are attracted to people who seem to be the same as us on some level because we can relate to them and their experiences.

Being able to build instant rapport is a hallmark of a charismatic person. It is the most important ingredient to creating new connections. It is the key that opens the door to new, meaningful relationships. When we meet someone new, we are both trying to see if we have a key that fits their door – if we have some kind of shared belief, experience, fear, or passion from which a bond can be built. When we find that key, it gives us enough trust to open the door and to begin to build a genuine bond with them.

Charismatic people are exceptional at building rapport because they are comfortable with themselves, actively listen to others, and have a broad range of personal experiences to draw from when looking for a key that will allow them to relate to someone new.

JAY LENO: A CASE STUDY IN BUILDING RAPPORT

If there is one skill a talk show host must have, it is the ability to instantly connect with other people in a way that gets them to share their stories. As the former host of "The Tonight Show," Jay Leno perfected this skill over his years hosting the show.

But being able to build rapport with the people populating his couch wasn't always enough. At one point, the show was losing the ratings war to "Late Night with

David Letterman" and the team at "The Tonight Show" needed to make changes to try to get back on top. One of the changes they made was to move some of the audience seating closer to the stage. This made it possible for Leno to walk over and shake audience members' hands on the way to his desk.

This may seem like a small and insignificant thing but it was one of the changes credited with boosting the show's ratings. It helped because it allowed Leno to build rapport with the studio audience right at the beginning of the show. Since the people in the studio audience were just like the people in the home audience, viewers responded as if he was shaking their hands too. They felt like they were part of the experience and that made them want to watch.

ESTABLISHING RAPPORT

Rapport is all about creating a connection. Whether you are at a networking event, a social gathering, or standing in line at a coffee shop, being able to quickly make a connection is a skill all charismatic people share. Here are five tips for building rapport:

Rapport-Building Tip #1:
SEEK COMMON GROUND

Creating these connections means starting conversations with people you don't know. This means that if you want to boost your charisma, you need to start by improving your mastery of small talk.

If you just groaned out loud, you are not alone.

Most people don't like small talk, but it is a necessary part of establishing and building rapport because, well, you have to start somewhere.

The goal of small talk is to find that common ground, to find some commonality between you and the other person from which you can create a connection. In order to do that, you need to learn more about the other person. This is why the best small talk involves asking open-ended questions that can't be answered with a simple yes or no.

For example, if you meet someone new at a business event and you ask them "Hasn't the weather been crazy this week?" they can simply say yes or no, effectively ending the conversation before it starts.

But, if you say, "What do you think about all the crazy weather we have had this week?" you are asking for more than a yes or a no. Even more importantly, in terms of creating rapport, you are letting this person know that you are interested in their opinion.

When the other person answers your question, they open up about some part of their life. In their response, you may be able to find that nugget of commonality that ties the two of you together.

For more techniques on how to master small talk, check out my book *Small Talk Hacks* on www.AkashKaria.com/SmallTalk

Rapport-Building Tip #2:
REMEMBER THE SWEETEST SOUND IN ANY LANGUAGE

Do you know the sweetest word in any language? It's that person's name. People's identity rests on their names, so remembering people's names goes a long way.

Can you remember a time when someone you met used your name in conversation?
How did it make you feel?

I know that every time someone new meets me and uses my name in conversation, it makes me feel that the other person finds me important enough to remember my name. It makes me like the other person more than I would otherwise.

Similarly, when you meet someone new, pay close attention when they tell you their name. And then use their name at least three times during the conversation. First at the beginning, then a couple of minutes later, and then finally when you are saying goodbye. Not only does this make the other person feel important, it also helps you remember that person's name for the next time you meet!

If you struggle to remember people's names, then use this technique (via Forbes - www.bit.ly/ForbesNames):

Make a vivid association between their name and something familiar to you. As you're silently saying to yourself his or her name, link the name with something familiar to you.

Darlene Price, author of Well Said! Presentations and Conversations That Get Results, suggests. "Caution: the more bizarre and exaggerated the visualization, the better," she says. "The other person will never know your image, so make it a memorable one."

For example, if the person's name is Jeff, you may pick a word that rhymes with it, like 'chef.'

"Visualize Jeff wearing a chef's hat, cooking in your kitchen, wearing a pot on his head (remember the more bizarre the better)," Price says. "Or link Jeff to a famous Jeff, such as the movie star Jeff Bridges; or use alliteration such as Jumping Jeff, Jolly Jeff, or Judge Jeff with respective appropriate images. It doesn't really matter what you use, so long as the association you choose effectively triggers recall of the person's name. You have to search in the moment to use something familiar. It's a simple trick and it's been proven to stick."

Rapport-Building Tip #3:
MIRROR AND MATCH

Another important part of establishing commonality is to make the other person feel like you are like them. Mirroring and matching is the best way to do this. This technique is used by salespeople and negotiators to create some common ground from which a connection can be made.

Here's how this works.

Let's say you are visiting a potential client who talks fast, laughs loud, and never seems to stop moving. You can create some common ground by mirroring his behavior and matching his tone and pace. If he laughs loudly, you laugh loudly too. If his tone changes because he is ready to get down to business, you change your tone too.

While you don't want to actually mimic the other person, which can feel contrived and may make them feel like you are making fun of them, matching their tone and pace and mirroring their body language will create a sense of sameness that encourages them to make a connection.

Rapport-Building Tip #4:
ASK FOR HELP

If you are struggling to find some open-ended question to ask and don't have a good reason to make yourself scarce in the next 10 minutes, another option you have for starting the conversation is to ask for help. The simplest example of this is to ask for the time, and then after getting the time transitioning into introducing yourself and asking about the other person (really cool and sneaky way to start a conversation, isn't it?). Everyone likes to be helpful and when you ask someone for assistance, you are making them feel important while starting a stealth conversation.

In fact, many people may not even realize that you are asking for help as a way to start a conversation with them. For people that really struggle with small talk, this can be a great way to make the first move that feels more comfortable than asking a stranger a random question out of the blue.

Here's an example:

> "Next time you're at a coffee shop with your
> laptop, you can ask anyone near you the innocent
> question, 'Is your internet working? Mine seems
> really slow…' You may have the fastest Internet
> connection in the world, but that doesn't matter.
> Your sole mission is to start the conversation. If
> you successfully ignite a conversation, in the end,
> no one will care or remember how it started." –
> Via LifeHack (www.bit.ly/ConversationHack)

What you ask for help with is not important, only the fact
that you ask and that they respond. Here are a couple of
examples, courtesy of LifeHack
(www.bit.ly/ConversationHack):

> At a convention or event: "This food looks
> good…do you think we can start eating yet?"

> Near a festival: "I wonder what's going on down
> there?"

> Concert or convention: "Do you know when
> ____ is supposed to start?"

> In the city: "Do you know where I can find a
> Verizon store around here? Mine is giving me
> issues…"

Rapport-Building Tip #5:
USE COMMONALITY TO CONNECT

Once you find that nugget of common ground, you have what you need to instantly create the connection we refer to as rapport. All you need to do is show the other person the common ground you have found by saying something like....

"I can relate to that because..."

"I totally understand what you mean because...."

"I had something similar happen when I..."

"I know how that feels because..."

Each of these statements, when followed by a story relating your personal experience, tells the other person that you get them because you have been through what they have been through. You understand how they feel because you have felt that way too.

Instant connection, rapport established!

IN A NUTSHELL

So in social situations like business conferences, networking events, parties, etc., use the following tips to quickly find the common ground you need to establish rapport:

- Make sure you always use open-ended questions when seeking to start a conversation.

- If you don't have a good question, ask for help.

- Use the person's name in conversation to create a deeper bond.

- When you find that nugget of commonality, use rapport building language like "I can relate…" to establish a connection.

Chapter Four

SIX TECHNIQUES FOR CREATING LIKABILITY

"People like people who like them."
Kare Anderson

When it comes to the way people perceive you, likability matters. It doesn't matter how powerful you are or how passionate you are or even whether or not you have a perfectly positive attitude – if they don't like you, they won't trust you, they won't believe you, and they won't want to be around you. This is why likability is the X factor when it comes to charisma.

People create connections where there is common ground, and they are drawn to people they like. You can see this in everything from how people choose the person who sells them insurance to who gets hired for a job. Even when we think we are making a rational decision based on facts and evidence, we are usually picking the person we like the most, regardless of those facts and evidence.

Research supports this. One study showed that likability was more important than job experience, education, and qualifications when it came to hiring decisions. The bottom line is that we like doing business with people who are pleasant, helpful, willing, and well...that we like.

TOM HANKS: A CASE STUDY IN LIKABILITY

There is no question that Tom Hanks is likable, especially since he was voted the World's Most Likable Man, which is why you can learn a lot about the likability factor from looking at who he is and how he lives his life.

For starters, he is handsome, but in an everyman sort of way rather than a "sexiest man alive" kind of way. He has never been a heartthrob in the traditional sense, which makes him seem like he could be your father, brother, husband, or best friend. People like him because they can relate to him.

Even though he is past 50, he still has a boyish charm and a mischievous side that people find endearing. When he meets with reporters, he often spends as much time learning about them as he does talking about himself. He is the definition of down-to-earth despite being one of the biggest movie stars on the planet. People like him because being famous doesn't make him think he is better than other people.

He has a genuinely positive attitude about life, telling one reporter that he believes 80% of people are honest, trustworthy, and basically good at heart. He is polite and courteous with fans and the media. He is a nice guy in a world where not being nice gets you more press. From his lack of pretense to his down-home charm, Tom Hanks provides a template for likability that anyone can learn from.

BEING MORE LIKABLE

No matter who you are or what you do, being likable matters. Jobs, relationships, and all kinds of opportunities come to us through other people, and people only pass those things along to the people they like. It won't matter how much money you have or how good you look, you will never be charismatic if you can't get people to like you. To become more likable, use the following tips:

Likability Tip #1:
BE POSITIVE

The most important thing you must do in order to be more likable is foster a positive attitude. While the world is not always a happy place and there are lots of things to be negative about, no one likes to be around negative energy. But those people who remain positive, even when times are dark and the world feels like a dire place to be, are the beacons of light that draw others out of all that negativity. An article on *Business Insider* by Richard Feloni on the "14 Habits of Exceptionally Likable People" echoes this sentiment:

> "It's often easier to give into cynicism, but those who choose to be positive set themselves up for success and have better reputations." – Via Business Insider (www.bit.ly/14Habits)

You can become one of those people that simply radiate positivity by developing these important skills:

A – FLIP THE SWITCH

Whenever you start to get down and feel negative, shift your focus to a similar situation that had a positive outcome. Rather than dwelling on everything that isn't going right, focus on what has gone right in the past as a reminder that success is always within your reach. Choosing to switch from focusing on the bad to focusing on the good will increase the positive energy in everything you do.

For example, let's say you are a guy out on the town with some friends and after striking out with two women you are feeling pretty down. Rather than wallowing in that rejection, refocus your thoughts on a time when a girl said yes and use this positive energy to lift you up.

B – TAKE CONTROL

When things are not going well it is easy to feel like there is nothing you can do to make things better or to feel better yourself. But this is likely to only increase your negativity. The truth is negativity is a choice. So is being positive. Take control of your thoughts and choose to look on the bright side or to seek out the silver lining.

For example, let's say you have been to visit 10 potential clients this week without getting anyone to sign. You feel like you will never make a sale again. Continuing to think like that only makes that outcome more likely. Instead, choose not to focus on the sales you didn't get and to focus on what you can do to get the next sale or the one after that.

Likability Tip #2:
POLITENESS PAYS

There is a reason that your mother was so adamant that you learn to say please and thank you – it matters when you are out in the world interacting with other people. The simple act of acknowledging the kindness or effort of others with a thank-you can change your life.

To understand why this is so important, let's look at two scenarios to see who comes across more likable.

Person A is pretty, funny, and successful. She has a great smile but she saves it for those people she needs to charm and persuade at work. She gets her morning coffee at the same place and same time every morning where she is brisk with the clerk or cashier, rarely bothering to look up from her phone to acknowledge them as she gives them her order. When her coffee is ready, she grabs it from the clerk without even glancing their way, and heads for the door.

Person B is also pretty, funny, and successful. She has a great smile too but she shows it to as many people as she can every day. She gets her morning coffee at the same place and at the same time as Person A. When it's her turn at the counter, she says good morning to the cashier and smiles when she uses their name. She knows all the cashiers' names because she is there at the same time every day.

While they make her coffee she asks after their mothers or their husbands or their children, depending on whom she is talking to because she knows all those things too. She thinks it is important to get to know the people who make sure she has a delicious hot cup of coffee every morning to start her day. When her coffee is ready, she smiles and says, "Thank you!" and "Have a great day!" before she takes her coffee and heads to the door.

Which of these customers are more likely to get the special customer appreciation discount from the clerks? Person B didn't really go out of her way to get the people who work in the coffee shop to like her, she was simply polite and courteous.

Acknowledging the cashier, interacting with the staff, smiling, and saying thanks were simple things but they reaped big rewards, especially on the day that the shop ran out of the coffee both of these women drank every day. The clerks set aside one cup when they started to run low and it didn't go to Person A.

Being polite and courteous just takes practice. Make it a point to say "please," "thank you," and "you're welcome" when appropriate and to acknowledge anyone you interact with, even the coffeehouse cashier or the subway token taker.

Whenever possible, do the right things for other people. This includes things like holding open the door, stopping to let someone cross the street, giving up your seat on the subway, or helping someone carry a heavy load to their car.

Be aware of the people around you and respect their space. This means paying attention to where you are walking so you don't walk in front of someone or stop suddenly when they are walking behind you. Keep your phone conversations as quiet as possible and turn off the sound on your phone and other devices. No one needs to hear you playing Candy Crush all the way home from work!

Likability Tip #3:
THE NO-BRAINER HONESTY RULE

While this might seem like a no-brainer, in today's world it is not. It is a little sad that people have to be told to be honest and tell the truth if they want other people to like them, but that is the world we live in. Being honest is hard work, especially when not being honest might serve you better.

But truth will almost always come out and in order to like you, people need to trust you. Be honest because being caught in a lie will always do more damage than coming clean right out of the gate.

Likability Tip #4:
CONFIDENT, NOT COCKY

There is a fine line between walking into a room with a straight back and a head held high in a way that lets everyone know you are confident and doing the same thing with a little swagger and a slight grin that sends a completely different, much less likable message. People with charisma know how to walk that line.

When you meet someone new, extend your hand first, smile, and take a step toward them. While some would caution that you are "giving up your power position" by doing this, you don't need all that posturing to be powerful if the people you are interacting with like you. Being likable is a very powerful thing all by itself.

Always remember that being confident in your abilities does not require you to denigrate or degrade the abilities of others. Be confident in who you are, not in who you are when compared with someone else.

Likability Tip #5:
THE POWER OF QUIET

Well, be quiet about yourself at least. If you want people to like you, let them tell you about the things they love. Ask open-ended questions and then stop talking so they can tell you about themselves and what matters to them. Be part of the conversation, just not the subject of it.

The next time you meet someone new, try this tactic.

Ask an open-ended question and then really listen to the answer.

Find the most interesting thing they said and ask more about that.

Ask how they did something, why they made that choice, or who they had that experience with.

Ask for more details.

Learn as much as you can about their experiences and about what they learned from that experience.

They will like you because you were quiet and listened to them but they will like you even more because you were interested in hearing more than just their first response.

Likability Tip #6:
THE "HA-HA" TECHNIQUE

While it is important to be professional in some circumstances, there is always room for a little humor in every situation. Everyone likes someone with a sense of humor.

This doesn't mean that you turn yourself into the grown-up version of the class clown who is willing to do anything for a laugh. It means remembering that laughter is healthy and that people love to laugh and, well, sometimes funny things happen. And that it is okay to laugh when they do.
People like to laugh and they like the people who make them laugh and the ones that make them feel that

laughing is okay. Be both of those people and likability won't be a problem. To develop a sense of humor, look at all the humorous things that have happened to you in your life. Some examples from my life (remember, there is a funny side to every story!) include:

- Managing to sneak up to the president's helicopter when I was younger so I could say hello to him, only to be tackled by his bodyguards.

- How I received my letter from Harvard on April Fool's Day and kept expecting them to send a "Ha-ha, we fooled you!" mail – which never came!

- The fact that I don't drink alcohol even when I go to parties and clubs, and women always approach me and chat me up wondering why I'm not drinking.

- Somehow I signed up and got entry into a women-only networking event (a fact I realized only after I entered the networking event!).

If you search hard enough, you'll find humorous incidents in your life too – you just have to look at everything from a lighthearted perspective.

Having a sense of humor also means being able to confidently accept everything that comes your way and harmlessly deflect it with humor. Let me give you an example.

Recently, I went to the cinema with a female and a male friend of mine. While grabbing a quick dinner before the movie, my female friend noticed that my shirtsleeve was slightly ripped, so she asked, "Why is your shirtsleeve ripped?" to which I replied, "It gives women an excuse to put their hands on my biceps!"

The line elicited laughter from all of us.

Why?

Because it was an unexpected, lighthearted and fun response to the question. Sure, I could have defended why my sleeve was ripped by saying, "I was shopping at the supermarket when I accidently ripped my shirt on a corner of steel shelf," but instead I accepted that my shirt was ripped and played along those lines.

Similarly, when I attended the women-only networking event, one of the women asked me, "What are you doing at this women-only event?" I could have defended myself by saying, "Well, I signed up accidentally." Instead I accepted what she was saying and went along with it by saying, "It's a great place to meet women!" Again, we both shared a laugh.

Next time someone says something, don't go for the most obvious answer. Instead, go along with the basic premise of what they are saying and use exaggeration and self-deprecation to turn the premise into a setup for laughter. Of course this will take practice, but keep at it.

Also observe comedians such as Russell Peters, Chris Rock and Trevor Noah, and pay attention to what they say that makes you laugh. This simple exercise will allow you to appreciate the humor in small daily things and over time you too will begin to become a more humorous person.

IN A NUTSHELL

e guidelines below, you will come across
ever you are interacting socially with other
people.

- Be positive.

- Be polite and courteous.

- Be honest.

- Be confident, not cocky.

- Be quiet.

- Have a sense of humor.

Chapter Five

THE ART OF ACTIVE LISTENING

"Listening is a magnetic and strange thing, a creative force. The friends who listen to us are the ones we move toward. When we are listened to, it creates us, makes us unfold and expand."
Karl A. Menniger

If there is one thing that separates the people who are charismatic from the people who wish they were charismatic, it has to be how much they talk. Those who haven't figured out the secret to having more charisma often confuse being charismatic with being the star of the show. They go out of their way to tell funny, engaging stories and do what they can to be the life of the party.

But what they don't realize is that charismatic people listen more than they talk. They listen actively, which keeps them engaged with the other person or people. They listen because this shows interest in the other person and what they are saying. They listen because it makes other people feel important. According to an article on the "14 Habits of Exceptionally Likable People" on Business Insider (www.bit.ly/14Habits), "The most likable people use conversations as an opportunity to learn about another person and give them time to talk."

Other people will always be more interested in you if you are interested in them. This is because we humans are always seeking commonality; we are always searching for common ground, shared experiences, and others we can connect to.

You cannot find that common ground or form the connection that comes from finding it if you are the only one who is talking.

OPRAH WINFREY: A CASE STUDY IN ACTIVE LISTENING

Oprah Winfrey hosted the most popular talk show in history for more than two decades and is considered by many to be the most influential woman in the world. People flocked to her show, buy products she recommends, and treat her advice and guidance as gospel truth. She has interviewed people from across the societal spectrum from Michael Jackson and Tom Cruise to Sarah

Ferguson and Barack Obama to everyday Joes and Janes with interesting stories to share.

Oprah is considered the Queen of All Media and remains incredibly influential almost 5 years after her award-winning show went off the air. One of the reasons she has had such monumental success is because she knows how to listen.

To understand the power of active listening all you need to do is watch Oprah interview a guest, any guest. She treats them all the same. She treats them all as though they are the most important person she could be talking to at that moment. Her attention is focused, which is clearly communicated through her facial expression and body language.

She is interacting with her guest, even when she isn't asking questions. Her head nods in silent agreement at just the right time, a smile plays across her face at a humorous anecdote, sadness fills her eyes as her guest tears up. These are the hallmarks of an expert at active listening.

BECOMING AN ACTIVE LISTENER

Charismatic people are curious and interested in other people. This desire to learn more about another person and the ability to be deeply interested in almost anyone are two of the reasons people are so drawn to those with lots of charisma. At the heart of both of those reasons is the ability to actively listen. Here are tips to help you with active listening:

Active Listening Tip #1:
LISTEN WITH YOUR WHOLE BODY

Most people hear with their ears but charismatic people actively listen with their whole body. They picture what the person is talking about in their mind, they smile, they nod, they make eye contact; in short, they react, using nonverbal body language which lets the person know they are interested, invested, and actually listening to every word.

When you are in a meeting or participating in an interview, listen closely so that you can nod, smile, laugh, sigh, shift, etc., at appropriate times. These physical cues tell the speaker you are listening to their words and that you care about what they are saying.

Active Listening Tip #2:
COMMISERATE AND EMPATHIZE

When it is time for you to say something, limit your comments to those that are empathetic and supportive.

For example, if your coworker is having a really tough week and asks you to have lunch because she needs someone to talk to, let her talk. Offer support and empathy by saying things like…

"That sounds rough, how are you holding up?"

"I can't imagine how hard this is for you; do you have any help at home?"

"It isn't fair that you have to go through this, but I know you are strong and you will pull through."

Active Listening Tip #3:
DON'T TRY TO HELP

…Unless they ask for help. What most of us do when we listen to another person talk about a problem is to jump in and try to solve it (this is especially true of men). We can't wait to share our experiences and advice. But most of the time when we try to do this we turn things around and make the conversation about us, rather than keeping the focus on them.

We think we are being helpful, but unless the other person specifically asks for advice or specifically asks for help, you need to give them only what they asked for – someone to listen.

Active Listening Tip #4:
LISTEN UNTIL THEY ARE DONE TALKING

Another frequent mistake people make is to stop listening after the first few words because they are focused on how they will respond. Instead of being present and paying attention, they are mentally formulating their own response.

Instead, maintain your focus on what others are saying without judging, refuting, interrupting, or responding until they are done. If you need time to formulate your response, you can take that time before you respond.

For example, using the example of your harried coworker from above, imagine how she would feel if she started telling you about her problem and you cut her off after a couple minutes because you think you know what she is going to say and you think she is wrong.

At a minimum, she isn't likely to come to you the next time she needs someone to talk to. But you could upset her, hurt her feelings, make her feel stupid, make her mad, etc. And none of those responses are the kind of responses charismatic people get from the people in their lives.

Active Listening Tip #5:
CLARIFY, PARAPHRASE, OR REFLECT

Rather than responding by judging the person or trying to fix their problem, show them you are really listening by asking clarifying questions or asking the person to reflect on the experience they are telling you about.

Examples of clarifying questions are:

"When you say it is turning into a disaster, what does that actually mean?"

"If I heard you correctly..."

"When did this start?"

"Tell me more about..."

You can also paraphrase what the person said, which means repeating it back to them in your own words. This shows them you are interested and listening without redirecting the conversation.

Asking questions that encourage the person to reflect on what they said or on the experience they are relaying is also an important active listening skill. Examples of these kinds of questions are:

"What got you through that difficult time?"

"What did you learn from that experience?"

"What was the best part of that experience?"

"Looking back, would you do anything differently?"

Active Listening Tip #6:
LEARN TO SHUT OUT DISTRACTIONS

The world is a busy, noisy, active place and our attention spans are rarely up to the task of filtering out all that external stimuli in order to maintain focused attention. But in order to become a better listener, you need to learn how to shut out the distractions that will continually pull your attention from the person speaking.

Common distractions include the hums and beeps of electronics and machines that constantly surround us; the environmental conditions around us like smells, heat, cold, or wind, and the swirl of our own thoughts inside our brains. With so many things vying for our limited attention, you might feel like keeping your focus is impossible.

But it can be done.

The first challenge is to catch your attention slipping. Often when you become distracted, you won't even realize it for seconds or even minutes. You just suddenly become aware that you have no idea what the other person is talking about.

To avoid this, you need to learn to catch the slip when it happens. If you are using the other active listening tips in this chapter, this should be easy. When you are really listening to someone, the drift in your attention will be more noticeable. When you catch that drift, use the paraphrasing technique above to make sure you haven't missed anything.

But if you are at a networking event where the noise level is making it difficult to concentrate, it's okay to let the other person know you are having trouble focusing. Simply explain that you are really interested in what they are saying but the noise in the room is making it difficult to stay focused. Ask if you can move to another location.

This approach will work regardless of the situation. Another person is always going to be more receptive to you asking to change venue when you are making the request because you want to be able to focus on what they are saying.

IN A NUTSHELL

Learn to be a better listener and you will charm everyone you meet because you will make them feel important and interesting simply by giving them a little of your attention.

- Listen with your whole body.

- Commiserate and empathize.

- Don't try to help.

- Listen until they are done talking.

- Clarify, paraphrase, or reflect.

- Learn to shut out distractions.

Chapter Six

HOW TO BE INTERESTING

"Don't fear failure so much that you refuse to try new things. The saddest summary of a life contains three descriptions: could have, might have, and should have."
Unknown

If you want to be more charismatic, you need to focus on being interesting as well. Interesting people are magnetic. They draw people towards them because people want to know more about them. They live interesting lives, which means they have great stories. They are well-traveled, well read, and have invested the time and energy required to formulate educated opinions. When it comes to charisma, interesting often equals attractive.

We are more attracted to people who are intriguing and engaging because they feed our need for new information, entertainment, and novel experiences. Our brains have pretty short attention spans, which is why we are always on the lookout for something new to think about, see, hear, discover, discuss, or learn. This is why we are so attracted to interesting people regardless of their physical attributes.

Being interesting is another thing that sets apart those who have mastered charisma from those who haven't. Most people try to hide the more unusual, intriguing, quirky things about themselves because they want to fit in and seem normal. But normal is average and average is boring. If you want people to be drawn to you, boring won't do.

BILL CLINTON: A CASE STUDY IN BEING INTERESTING

There is no question that former President Bill Clinton has led an interesting life. From his humble roots in Arkansas to his surprising victory over incumbent President George H.W. Bush in 1992 to the scandal that led to him being only the second president to be impeached in the history of the country, he has stories to tell. And when it comes to telling stories, there aren't many better than Mr. Clinton.

His 2012 speech at the Democratic Convention is the perfect example of how President Clinton can take even complicated, wonky policy information and weave it into an interesting tale that educates and enlightens without ever making his listeners feel as though he is talking down to them. His ability to take complex concepts and use his innate knack as a storyteller to present them in a way that everyone can relate to is what makes him such a charismatic communicator.

HOW TO BE MORE INTERESTING

Charismatic people have interesting lives. They are the explorers, the inventors, the adventurers, and the doers that are out there living the lives the rest of us only wish we were living. But you don't have to be base-jumping off the Empire State Building to be the kind of interesting that other people are drawn toward. You just need to do things and then share them with other people. Here are four tips to help you become more interesting:

How to Be Interesting Tip #1
LIVE AN INTERESTING LIFE

If you want to be more interesting you are going to have to get off the couch and out of the office and go out into the world to do something more than what you are doing right now. Here are some of the things you can do to up the interesting quotient in your life.

- Make a list of at least 10 things you have never done (but have always wished to do) and then pick one and go do it right now.

- Make plans with other people to do the other nine.

- Eat dinner at a new restaurant once every two weeks.

- Take a walk in a different part of your city once a month.

- Go on a road trip.

- Learn to do something new like karate or yoga or cooking.

- Make a new friend every month for a year.

- Say yes when someone asks you to do something exciting or adventurous with them.

The list is endless. The point is that you are never going to have a more interesting life if you aren't out there doing new and interesting things. Get off the couch and go!

How to Be Interesting Tip #2:
BE DIFFERENT

If you are doing the same things as everyone else you won't be interesting, you will be normal. This means that going to the trendiest restaurants isn't going to make you interesting. In order to stand out from the crowd and give off the vibe that makes people want to know what you did last week, you have to do things that are different from what other people do.

The easiest way to do this is to ask friends, coworkers, and acquaintances for ideas of things that everyone does in the area where you work and live.

Then ask the same people what no one ever does.

Take your two lists and swap them.

If it is something everyone does, like taking picnics to Central Park, you are never going to do it.

If it is something almost no one does, like spending a Saturday night at the planetarium, add that to your list of things you want to do.

Go against the grain and do things that are unexpected. That is what will make you interesting.

How to Be Interesting Tip #3
LEARN TO TELL A GREAT STORY

Stories are the way we experience the world vicariously through other people, which means the people who can tell a great story will always be the most interesting among us. It won't matter if you are para-gliding through the Amazon in order to deliver vaccines to tribal babies if you can't turn that interesting experience into a sharable anecdote for others to devour.

Once you have some new and interesting life experiences to impart, use these storytelling tips to make your story as interesting as possible.

- **Share the details.** When it comes to storytelling, details are king. Instead of saying, "The beach was beautiful!" add more details by saying, "The beach was beautiful – the water was so clear you could see the fish swimming in it. And the weather was just gorgeous – sunny but with a cool breeze!" Add details that paint pictures in your listeners' minds and transport them into your story.

- **Highlight the humorous.** Everyone likes to laugh and if you can retell your story in a way that has highlights of humor, it will be even more interesting and memorable to those listening.

- **Make it relevant.** Even if the experience you are sharing happened a decade ago, you can make it relevant by tying it to something that is happening in the world right now.

- **Be enthusiastic!** When telling your story, share it with enthusiasm. Make a conscious decision to be enthusiastic – let your voice and your facial expressions and gestures reflect your enthusiasm. When you are enthusiastic, your listeners will be too!

How to Be Interesting Tip #4
HAVE THREE GREAT STORIES READY TO TELL

So you have done some interesting things that will make some good stories. Now you need to turn those experiences into relatable, relevant stories that you can use in social situations. Professional comedians and politicians never get on stage without writing, reviewing, and practicing their act or their speech. Make sure you don't go "on" without taking the time to figure out the best way to tell your story, just like the professionals.

You should do this for at least three stories so that you always have three stories you know you are ready to tell. This lets you pick the story that is most appropriate for the situation and ensures you have more than one thing to talk about in any social situation.

When choosing which stories you want to develop and practice, pick stories that center around other people rather than things or places (without people). Stories about other people are the most impactful and interesting to the general public.

IN A NUTSHELL

Interesting lives take effort. Create a more interesting life and then share it with the world by:

- Making sure you live an interesting life.

- Being different.

- Learning to tell a great story.

- Prepping your stories ahead of time.

Chapter Seven

THE POWER OF AUTHENTICITY

"Always be a first-rate version of yourself and not a second-rate version of someone else."
Judy Garland

If there is one personality trait that serves as the foundation of a charismatic personality, it is authenticity. In order to embody each of the characteristics of charismatic people, you must inspire others to believe in you. And getting others to believe IN you means they first need to believe you, which requires that you come across as authentic.

But what does that actually mean?

Authenticity is achieved when you are true to who you are. The tools in this book are designed not to change who you are, but to make you the best version of you that you can be. You are not putting on airs. You are not pretending to be something you are not. You own your strengths and weaknesses.

You know what makes you great and where you are prone to falter. You live according to the values you hold dear, regardless of any pressure from external sources to be different. People believe what you say because they can tell that you believe what you say. People believe in you because they can tell that you believe in yourself.

Authenticity means being comfortable enough with yourself that you don't feel the need to put on a mask to please others. It is empowering for you, but it is also empowering and inspirational for others. When you are true to yourself, you tell the people around you that it's okay to be yourself, warts and all, which gives them permission to be true to themselves as well.

Whether you are trying to win someone's trust, create new connections, build stronger bonds, or simply win that sale, there is nothing more powerful, nothing more persuasive than simply being who you are and letting that grounded feeling and your message win the day.

NELSON MANDELA: A CASE STUDY IN AUTHENTICITY

If you look across the world of great leaders, big thinkers, and charismatic celebrities, one person stands above the rest when you consider the trait of authenticity – the late Nelson Mandela, freedom fighter, apartheid ender, and former president of South Africa. Few people in history embody the idea of being authentic like President Mandela.

After being arrested for fighting against the apartheid regime, he spent 27 years in prison because he stood by what he believed in and refused to give up his fight. He was offered his freedom several times during his incarceration in exchange for his promise to give up the fight, but he refused. He believed that apartheid was wrong and he lived his truth, even when doing so required great personal sacrifice.

This is the essence of authenticity – believing your truth and then living it. Mandela was released, the apartheid regime ended, and when the people of South Africa looked for the leader they would need to build a new South Africa, Mandela was the obvious choice. It was his belief in standing up for what he thought was right that inspired others to join that fight. It was his willingness to live those values, even if that meant living in a cell, which encouraged others.

While Mandela embodied other charismatic traits, skills, and characteristics, it was his authenticity that took him from that prison cell to the height of South African politics and world admiration.

ACHIEVING AUTHENTICITY

Not everyone can be Nelson Mandela. But you don't need to be a Mandela to achieve a level of authenticity that will strengthen your persona, feed your passion, enhance your positivity, and increase your overall charisma.

The following tips, techniques, and tactics will help you become more authentic and help your authenticity show through when you are interacting with others.

Authenticity Tip #1
SETTLE INTO YOUR OWN SKIN

Okay, that might sound a little strange but part of being authentic is being really comfortable in your own skin. Most of us spend a lot of time trying to hide the things we don't like about ourselves from others while berating ourselves for not being perfect. But what we should be doing is celebrating the good and accepting the bad. This is, after all, what we do with our friends, spouses, and family members.

So, take a little time to peek into the dark corners and locked closets where all the things you are the most insecure about reside. Bring them out, dust them off and spend some time getting to know them a little better. Some of them are likely to be fears – such as failing, looking bad, or losing everything. Others might be things you don't like about yourself or wish you could be better at, like your body shape or your social skills.

Let them out of their hiding spaces without judging them and then treat them as you would treat a friend. See if there is a solution. Be supportive. But most importantly, be accepting that this is a part of you.

Now, work on changing the things you can change and let go of any judgments about the rest. Once you stop trying to hide parts of yourself away from the world, you will automatically come across as more authentic to the people you interact with.

Authenticity Tip #2
FALL A LITTLE IN LOVE WITH YOURSELF

Okay, that sounds a little strange too, but it is what you need to do.

How will other people believe that you are great if you don't?

It's time to embrace all the wonderful and amazing things that make you who you are.

Start by making a list of your favorite things about yourself. Write down as many as you can think of. Next, make a list of all your strengths and your talents. Finish it off by adding all the things you have accomplished in your life.

Now, go grab a cup of coffee and sit down and read both lists.

You are pretty amazing, aren't you?

As you look at the list, ask yourself what you would think if this were a list of someone else's accomplishments.

Would you be impressed by the things on the list if they belonged to another person?

The goal here is not to convince you that you are more amazing than others or to make you into an overconfident oaf. It isn't about competing with someone else to be the most amazing at something. It is about acknowledging the best things about you so you aren't trying to hide or diminish or disregard those parts of yourself.

Authenticity is about being comfortable with who you are, both the good and the bad.

Authenticity Tip #3
VALIDATE YOUR VALUES

At its heart, authenticity is about living a life aligned with your values. It means standing up for what you believe in, whatever the cost. Just like Nelson Mandela.

But in order to do that, you need to know what you value and understand which beliefs are worth standing up for.

Start by looking at the list of words below and writing down those that speak to you. You can also add any other value words to your list that speak to you if they aren't listed here:

- Acceptance
- Accomplishment
- Accountability
- Adventure
- Altruism
- Balance
- Compassion
- Courage
- Creativity
- Dependability
- Enthusiasm
- Fidelity
- Freedom
- Generosity

- Gratitude
- Humility
- Intelligence
- Kindness
- Perseverance
- Professionalism
- Self-control
- Warmth

Now rank these values in priority order. Take a little time to write some notes about what each of the top 10 values on your list mean to you.

Now, for each of those top 10, answer the following questions:

- What am I doing today to live aligned with this value?

- What am I doing today that is not aligned with this value?

- What changes am I willing to commit to making to become more aligned with this value?

Now you have a list of your core values and an action plan for making the changes in your life that will bring you into better alignment with those values.

When you live aligned to your values, you are walking the walk. People can sense this about you and they will see you as more trustworthy and worthy of respect.

IN A NUTSHELL

Charisma is about attracting, intriguing, influencing, persuading, and connecting with others. Nothing will enable you to do these things more successfully than simply being yourself.

So, get comfortable in your skin, fall a little in love with yourself, live your values, and you will be amazed at the way people interact and engage with you.

Chapter Eight

WRAP UP

"Shine with all you have. When someone tries to blow you out, just take their oxygen and burn brighter."
Katelyn S. Irons

We've covered a lot of tools and techniques for achieving success in this tiny book. This chapter will serve as a useful summary of some of the most important tools and techniques covered in the book.

1 – Charm them with inviting eyes. Use the eye-color technique to hold longer-than-usual eye contact with people.

2 – When in groups, use the one thought, one person technique to establish a connection with everyone in the group.

3 – Perfect your posture by standing up and sitting up straight because this shows you as being a confident, self-assured person.

4 – Master the handshake to make a stellar first impression.

5 – Keep an open body-posture (rather than a closed one) to come off as more approachable and inviting.

6 – When talking to people, pay attention to their body language to see how they respond, and adjust your tactics accordingly.

7 – Respect people's personal space.

8 – Use your gestures naturally to show what you're saying.

9 – Smile – all the way to your eyes.

10 – Seek common ground when chatting to make people feel at ease and draw them out of their shell.

11 – Use open-ended questions when starting up a conversation.

12 – If you don't have a good question, ask for help to sneakily and subtly start up a conversation.

13 – When you find a nugget of commonality, use rapport-building language such as "I can relate..." to establish a connection.

14 – Use the person's name in conversation at least three times to build a deeper bond with the person you're speaking with.

15 – Use mirroring and matching to build rapport.

16 – Be a positive, upbeat person because people flock to positive energy.

17 – Remember that politeness and honesty pay off in the long run.

18 – Be confident, but not cocky.

19 – Be part of the conversation, not just the subject of it.

20 – Keep some humorous stories in mind to share to keep the conversation entertaining.

21 – Develop your wit and sense of humor by learning to accept and add onto whatever is being said (instead of defending or deflecting it).

22 – Study your favorite comedians to gain a deeper appreciation of how to turn simple, daily events into humorous anecdotes.

23 – Use active-listening techniques to make the other person feel that they are the most important person in the room, and in return they will give you the same attention.

24 – Listen with your whole body.

25 – Commiserate and empathize.

26 – Don't try to help – just listen!

27 – Listen until the other person is done talking instead of mentally formulating your own response while they are still speaking.

28 – Clarify, paraphrase, or reflect to show the other person that you are paying attention.

29 – Learn to shut out distractions.

30 – Become a more interesting person by leading a more interesting life: Make a list of at least 10 things you have never done (but have always wished to do) and then pick one and go do it right now.

31 – Have three great stories ready to tell.

32 – Share the details of the story to transport capture your listener's imagination.

33 – Highlight the humorous in the story.

34 – Make a conscious decision to be enthusiastic when sharing your story.

35 – Aim to become the best version of you that you can possibly be: get comfortable in your skin, fall a little in love with yourself, live your values.

Master these simple things and you will come across as a more likable, approachable, confident, and charismatic individual.

To unlocking your inner charisma,

Akash Karia
www.AkashKaria.com

P.S. – If you would like to download a print-ready PDF of these techniques, then head over to:
www.AkashKaria.com/CharismaDownload

QUESTIONS OR COMMENTS?

I'd love to hear your thoughts. Email me on:
Akash@AkashKaria.com

INTERESTED IN HAVING ME SPEAK AT YOUR NEXT EVENT?

I deliver high-impact keynotes and workshops on productivity, time management, success psychology and effective communication. Check out the full list of my training programs on www.AkashKaria.com/Speaking and reach me on akash@akashkaria.com to discuss how we can work together.

GRAB $297 WORTH OF FREE RESOURCES

Want to learn the small but powerful hacks to make you insanely productive?

Want to discover the scientifically proven techniques to ignite your influence?

Interested in mastering the art of public speaking and charisma?

Then head over to www.AkashKaria.com to grab your free "10X Success Toolkit" (free MP3s, eBooks and videos designed to unleash your excellence). Be sure to sign up for the newsletter and join over 11,800 of your peers to receive free, exclusive content that I don't share on my blog.

YOU MIGHT ALSO ENJOY

If you enjoyed this book, then check out Akash's other books:

SMALL TALK HACKS

"Akash Karia is a communications expert. He has the people skills to go with it. This book is easy to read and packed with tips and techniques that you can implement immediately.

This isn't just about talking. Akash covers non-verbal cues, questioning and listening techniques as well as how to improve your charisma. He then steps it up a notch and tells you how leverage these techniques and take it to the next level.

It doesn't matter if you're an introvert or an extrovert, a confident talker or not, this book will have takeaways for everyone."
~ **Alastair Macartney, BASE Jumping World Champion & Bestselling Author of Perfect Madness**

Grab the book here:
www.AkashKaria.com/SmallTalk

HOW SUCCESSFUL PEOPLE THINK DIFFERENTLY

"This book is packed with really wonderful mindsets, reframes, and psychology tips, all backed with references and real science. This is like the "best of the best" self-help tips. A quick read, but a thanksgiving feast of food for thought."

~ **Tim Brennan, #1 Bestselling Author of '1001 Chess Tactics'**

"How Successful People Think Differently is a quick, easy read packed with practical tips and easy-to-follow advice...This book is for anyone who wants to aim higher."

~ **Gillian Findlay**

"This short and deceptively simple book contains a distillation of many other self-help and 'success literature' books...Illustrated by many examples from real life and generously filled with scientific references and suggestions for further reading, this book is a 'must have' for anyone who wishes to better themselves in life."

~ **John Joyce, Author of "Masterpiece"**

"I was pleasantly surprised that I learned new tips from this book. It gave me great ideas on how to think differently and put tips into place to change habits and create a more successful life."
~ **Stacy Nichols**

Grab the book here:
www.AkashKaria.com/SuccessBook

PERSUASION PSYCHOLOGY: 26 POWERFUL TECHNIQUES TO PERSUADE ANYONE!

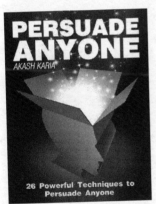

"I'm a huge fan of Akash's writing style and the way he can distill quite a complex subject into concise bite-sized points you can take away and convert into action. The book covers many different aspects of persuasion from the way you look to the words you use."
~ **Rob Cubbon, Author of "From Freelancer to Entrepreneur"**

Grab the book here:
www.AkashKaria.com/Persuasion

ANTI NEGATIVITY: HOW TO STOP NEGATIVE THINKING AND LEAD A POSITIVE LIFE

"Akash is a master at taking complex ideas and communicating with simplicity and brilliance. He honors your time by presenting what you need to know right away, and follows up with some excellent examples as reinforcement. If you're looking for some simple and effective ways to stop thinking negatively and a new season of positivity, definitely check out this book."
~ **Justin Morgan**

"This book was devoured in 2 - 3 hours! I could not wait for the additional tips to help work on the negative situations that get in my way. As a project manager dealing with managers that have tons of stress each day - my role for my clients it to help them make a transition from negative work environments and to figure out how to make it all better.So glad I have this book to review again and again."
~ **Elaine Jackson, BS, PMP, the Holistic Project Manager**

Grab the book here:
www.AkashKaria.com/AntiNegativity

READY, SET...PROCRASTINATE! 23 ANTI-PROCRASTINATION TOOLS DESIGNED TO HELP YOU STOP PUTTING THINGS OFF AND START GETTING THINGS DONE

"This is one book you should not delay reading! Having struggled with procrastination for much of my life, Akash Karia's book came like a breath of fresh air. He provides clear, practical advice on how to overcome the problem, but warns that you will need to work at it daily. This is a quick, very useful read and with 23 tips on offer, there will be several that you can identify with and implement for immediate results. If there is just one thing that you should not put off, it is reading this book."
~ **Gillian Findlay**

"This is a great manual on how to improve your every day productivity. The book gives very useful tips [that are] easy to follow and effective in their application."
~ **Rosalinda Scalia**

Grab the book here:
www.AkashKaria.com/AntiProcrastination

WANT MORE?

Then check out Akash's author-page on Amazon:
www.bit.ly/AkashKaria

ABOUT THE AUTHOR

Akash Karia is an award-winning speaker and peak productivity coach who has been ranked as one of the Top 3 speakers in Asia Pacific (JCI, 2015).

He is an in-demand international speaker who has spoken to a wide range of audiences including bankers in Hong Kong, students in Tanzania, governmental organizations in Dubai and yoga teachers in Thailand.

He is regularly sought-out by governments as well as businesses for his expertise on communication, motivation and peak performance psychology.

Akash currently lives in Tanzania where he works as the Chief Commercial Officer of a multi-million dollar company. When he is not writing or lazing around on a beach with a good book in his hands, he is available for speaking engagements and can be contacted through his website: **www.AkashKaria.com**

"Akash is THE best coach I've ever had!"
Eric Laughton, *Certified John Maxwell Trainer, United States*

"If you want to learn presentation skills, public speaking or just simply uncover excellence hidden inside of you or your teams, Akash Karia is the coach to go to."
Raju Mandhyan, *TV show host, Expat Insights, Philippines*

Voted as one of the "10 online entrepreneurs you need to know in 2015"
The Expressive Leader

Featured as one of the "top 9 [online] presentations of 2014"
AuthorStream.com

"I loved the two days with Akash, which were filled with useful information. His passion and enthusiasm made the classes fun and exciting."
Pricilla Alberd, *Australia*

"The two days in Akash's workshop have been excellent, very informative and packed with knowledge...tons of practical, ready to use techniques."
Edyte Peszlo, *Sales and Procurement Manager, Thailand*

"I found the course content very relatable and explained in a way that way not only very easy to understand but also incredibly interesting."
Hayley Mikkos-Martin, *Australia*

"Akash Karia is a fine public speaker who knows his subject very well. A rare talent who has much in store for you as an individual, and better yet, your organization."
Sherilyn Pang, *Business Reporter, Capital TV, Malaysia*

Grab your Free Success Toolkit:

www.AkashKaria.com/Free

Check out more Great books:

www.bit.ly/AkashKaria

Email for Speaking-Related Inquires:

akash@akashkaria.com / akash.speaker@gmail.com

Connect on LinkedIn:

www.LinkedIn.com/In/AkashKaria

Made in the USA
Middletown, DE
31 May 2016